WATERING THE SOUL

WATERING THE SOUL

COURTNEY PEPPERNELL

Andrews McMeel
PUBLISHING®

Acknowledgments

A special thank-you to all those involved in the creation of this book, including my team, my wife and family, Andrews McMeel Universal, and my wonderful illustrator Justin and his amazing ability to bring my visions to life. I have said this before and will gladly say it again: without all your efforts, reaching the finish line of any new book is not possible!

An extra-special thank-you to the team at Start the Wave for their inspirational mission to change the world. Their messages of kindness have helped inspire some poems in this book. To learn more about their mission and how you can help, head to www.startthewave.org.

And to the readers, as always, thank you for sharing and trusting your stories with me; there is no message, email, or comment unread. I keep them all in my heart, and they inspire me the most.

INSTAGRAM: @courtneypeppernell
TIKTOK: @courtneypeppernell
TWITTER: @CourtPeppernell
EMAIL: courtney@pepperbooks.org

It is in our darkest hour, when our soul feels most broken, that we are our strongest. For in the moments we feel we cannot go on, we learn we are braver than we ever thought we were.

This is the story of your soul and how it can be grown again.

There was an enchanted forest on the outskirts of a house I once called home. Past the wooden fence, down the little dirt path, deep, deep into the woods, I found myself one day. And here I met a small creature, made of leaves and light and joy. And the creature studied me thoughtfully, with a long inhale, as though it knew of my plight and my long-lost tale.

I knelt before the creature, my eyes filled with tears, and it asked me, "My friend, what is wrong? Why does your heart ache all night long?"

So, I said it was because I did not know who I was, in a world where so many people do. I said it was because I had truly lost all the things I'd ever known. How I felt so alone, no longer able to find shelter in my own soul, no longer able to find my way home.

And the creature thought for a long while before its eyes twinkled in a way that could make even the most broken believe. And it replied that it knew what to do and what I needed to find all my hopes and dreams. As the creature closed its eyes, a song began, a melody rising up from the forest floor, and soon the creature handed me a small seed and took my hand. "Follow me," it said, "and together, we will plant your soul once more."

So deeper into the woods we went, one foot in front of the other, until I planted the tiny seed of my soul into the soil and promised it the world in all its color. I promised I would water the seed and watch it grow, that I would stand beside it, no matter the season of rain or sun or snow. And the creature nodded, a smile upon its face, and said, "Remind yourself: to grow one's soul is a journey, not a race." And the creature handed me a recipe, a quest to find the ingredients and follow the steps, so I may find some much-needed clarity. In the fading sunlight, on that warm spring day, with my recipe in hand and a soul to grow, the creature had one last thing to say:

To grow means to leave much of what we believe to know behind. To move forward despite the darkness ahead, to slow down and breathe through every moment, to seek new paths, even if we are afraid. To find balance by embracing the silence, to forgive our mistakes, and to show our hearts and others more kindness. To look up and marvel at the sky and all its colors, to understand every road we walk is not alone but together. To have the courage to be patient with ourselves in the moments we need it most. To look within the deepest parts of ourselves, during the longest parts of the night, and search for our own light. To have the courage to understand that a seed is not grown with haste, and nor is becoming whole, that in each and every step, we find the meaning of watering the soul.

Let your journey begin . . .

How to WATER YOUR SOUL

Before you start:

Remember that no matter how many
times you veer off course, you can
always find your way back.

You will need:

Time, reflection & healing

Ingredients:

1 soul seeding
2 cups of slow breaths
1 tbsp of silence
3 cups of courage
1 bag of forgiveness
1 large packet of love
1 cup of solidarity
2 packets of patience/gratitude
4 cups of kindness
3 tsp of light

Steps:

1) Prepare your heart and mind, by taking a deep
   breath and slowing down your thoughts.
   Plant your soul seedling gently. Season with
   time and toss to coat.

2) Combine forgiveness, courage & kindness into
   a large bowl. Add silence and stir slowly
   until balanced.

3) In a second bowl, whisk solidarity and patience
   together. Once combined add to main bowl.
   Toss all ingredients together.

4) Pour mixture over planted seedling, water
   generously with love, and allow to shine.

5) Garnish with healing and reflection, and serve
   with gratitude on the side.

Enjoy!

Table of Steps

 low Down

There are many reasons
to race through life,
to hurry to the next moment
just as quickly as you burned
through every moment
before then.

But there is such beauty
in taking things in.
The way the leaves change
from season to season,
the sky at dusk and dawn,
a hand to hold
and someone to believe in.
Butterflies taking flight and
the glow of the moon at night.

If we slow down and take time
to see, we will truly be reminded
of the universe and all its beauty.

The way the moon
does not rush
from behind the clouds
but merely
waits for them to pass.
Be that with your thoughts.
Let your mind breathe.

You will always be learning, always be growing and taking things in. When someone calls you beautiful, there will always be a small part of your heart that wonders if that word is meant for you. It will always be meant for you. You are beautiful in the way you breathe and carry on, beautiful in the way you show courage to the days that are dark and long, beautiful in the way you are meant to be heard and embraced and known.

We view our life by running at it head-on. By always chasing after one emotion to the next. We try to avoid pain by never acknowledging it, by always covering it up with people or places or things to do. But that never allows the pain to heal. It never allows the wounds to close over and create the scars that tell our stories. If we stopped and acknowledged the pain, embraced the pain as an emotion that belongs to us, in the same way our happiness and joy belong to us, then we wouldn't be always running.

All my life
I have been stumbling
through moments,
desperate to reach the next,
without ever really finishing
the moment
I was currently in.

What I have learned by taking a moment to breathe:

i. Acceptance is a state of being.

ii. Listening isn't only hearing what you want to hear. Listening is acknowledging not all things will make sense, feel good, or be free from pain, but it is important to listen anyway. Listening leads to healing.

iii. Inhaling and exhaling is the soul's way of renewing. Each moment we take to stop and to breathe is healing.

iv. Spending time doing nothing is the best gift you can give yourself.

v. Small details often give us reason to love harder, work harder, and be at one with ourselves. By rushing, we often don't see those small details.

You will always have meaning. You mean something to the roses you admire, to the shore you stand upon, and to the salty air you breathe. You mean something to the sunset you marvel at and the smell of rain you inhale. You mean something to the sun and the moon and the stars, which shine for you, and to the universe, which wouldn't be the same without you. Finding meaning in this world and in this life can be as simple as slowing down and realizing that just by existing, you *already* hold so much meaning in this life.

Time slows when I think about my name wrapped around the base of her heart. Twisting and entwining, everlasting and binding. I could live for eternity in the warmth of her hands, the joy I feel from her laugh, and the hope I see in her smile. How she spends her days by the sea, gathering shells and dusting sand away from her shoes. She is a dream, comforting, alluring, and calming, every breath inside of me.

You cannot reach into the future and see what your heart feels any more than you can reach back into the past and change it. But you can hold your heart in the present. You can feel everything as each moment settles into existence. Listen to the way your heart feels in the present.

The uncertainty and the doubt are always going to be there. You will navigate these thoughts day in and day out. You will feel overwhelmed, like the noise of the world is too much. But this is why to slow down is to accept that life is filled with many feelings. Some are beautiful and others ugly, but they are all connected.

It was as though you had blinked
and suddenly the year was over.

You had just been watching
the countdown, sitting on your
living room floor, wine bottles all around,
laughing with the love of your life.

Then you read the book you said
you were always going to read,
and you finally went to the opera
and cried through the final act.

You bought seven new plants and
promised you would buy a new pair
of shoes. Those old loafers were worn.
You never did throw them out.

Then the love of your life left,
and for a while, it seemed like the world
had stopped right alongside you.
Only it hadn't.
The world carried on.

And then winter came, with snowdrops
on windowsills and trees baring it all
before spring returned, promising so
many new things: the way it always does.

And there was someone new and beautiful.
Someone who gently took your hand

and danced with you, whispered that there
was moonlight in your eyes.

You never thought you would make it.

But you learned something that year—
life could be more than surviving;
it could be lived.

This is the thing
about life and
all its chaos.

Most of us are
so eager
to get to the
next moment
or memory.

We want the
next adventure,
or journey,
or road to travel.

We want our
tomorrow
so swiftly
that so often
we forget to
be here *now*.

The magic happens
when you slow down
and take every moment
for what it is.

A gift.

I did fall in love.
Surely, wholeheartedly,
but not all at once.

It was patient, soft,
an everlasting feeling—
of forever.

When you find
such love,
there is a part
of your heart changed.

A part of your heart
that from that moment
forward
remains calm.

One morning, my eyes opened slowly, and the sunlight met me in a rush of joy and warmth. The light said to me, life has never been about all the things I could acquire or the days I had hastily filled with meaningless conversations. It was about slowing down, listening to the way a brook babbles over the land and into the stream, how the honeybees hum softly in the afternoon sunlight, how their little bellies gleam. The light reminded me to listen carefully, to rise above the notion of not enough, for if we don't live in the moment, we miss life's true message of humility.

When you are lost,
a well of grief grows,
overflowing with emotion.

It drowns all dreams,
hopes, and truths.

The constant struggle between
thoughts of reason,
the memories filled with ache,
the fear no one else will ever
understand you, all piled on
top of one another, so most
nights feel unbearable.

But just because the anxiety,
the loss, and the struggle tell you
that you are not strong or capable
or deserving of dreams coming true
does not mean it is the narrative
you belong to.

Your story is more than that.

More than feeling trapped within
the walls of your mind and
the fears in your heart.

Your story is in the way you
continue to carry on, each day,
every day, each year, every year.

There are these moments, right as the coffee is spilling, or the glass is falling, or you are tumbling over the hidden tree root, and it feels like time is still. As though you slowly see the seconds as they pull themselves together and you just know the ending isn't going to be pleasant. You are going to get hurt, or something is going to break. But it happens anyway, and you can't stop it. This is what heartbreak is. Those long, drawn-out seconds, between the falling and the ground, where it feels like no matter what you do, you can't stop the hurt from knocking the breath out of your lungs.

Stumbling is a part of life—
it happens.

You stumble, then you fall,
then you get back up again
and you stumble a little more.

Once in a while you fall hard,
and it takes a little more effort
to pull yourself back up again.

During these fragile moments,
it's the people who remind you
of your worth. Those are the ones
who care for you in a way
no one else ever will.

Your healing begins
on a day you look
in the mirror and
you don't recognize
the person staring back.

They are not the
person you have known
your whole life.
But an empty, withering
shadow.

You wonder where
that person has gone
and about the ache
that has pushed them
so far away.

And so you promise
this broken version
of yourself that
you'll find a way back,
just little steps day by day.

ad finally arrived,
noment of true clarity.
I was surrounded by beautiful
old trees, reaching for the sky
and the stars, every line and
every mark filled with old wisdom.

And they were whispering to themselves
and whispering to me that it is
important to go about life slowly.

To grow with purpose.

To take in every thought
and action with a deep
sense of empathy.

A whole lifetime, they say—and yet how fleeting our lives are.

Here is the story of someone I used to know—

She would hike every forest trail, without
stopping to admire all of nature in every detail.

She would drive every road, sunrise to sunset, without
noticing the sky and all its beauty, impossible to forget.

She would hold conversations along the way, without
pausing to ask the person if they were having a good day.

She would rush from one day to the next, eager
to move quickly through each and every step.
For a fear of choosing to spend her time sitting still
meant that, in the end, she would be left unfulfilled.

And at first, she did not see that living life like a race,
and spending every day consumed with such haste,
meant she had missed out on the beauty of dreaming
and learning what it truly means to be a human being.

That someone was me, and it took some time, but
eventually this is what I came to find—
for all the moments I've had
and all the things I've seen,
taking the time to truly be *here*
is the happiest I've ever been.

If you want to believe, then believe in honest conversations, believe in putting your best foot forward. Believe in the kindness of others, the warmth of the sun, the beauty of the ocean. Believe in slowing down and appreciating all of life's most intimate and tiny details. Believe in wonder, adventure, and the nostalgia of marshmallows around campfires. Believe in art galleries, bookstores, observatories, and the power of other people's stories.

 ake a Breath

We took the long way home, through back roads and over the mountain pass. You wanted to see the trees, glistening with frost as the day faded away. I had been grateful, because spending time with you was like listening to the rain right before I fall asleep. Being around you was like lying down in the middle of a meadow, arms wide, feeling the earth beneath my skin, knowing that a beautiful story was about to begin. You were quiet for so long, eyes glistening in the sunlight, watching the mountains in the distance. "Thank you," you had then said and reached across to take my hand in yours. I had shrugged and asked what for as you continued to stare out the window. And after a moment and a long exhale, you said, "Because, with you, I can finally breathe."

Be conscious of every breath
that you inhale and exhale.

Feel the way your chest
rises and falls,
the way a current moves
through your body.

Imagine yourself as rising mountains,
the glowing sun, the running river.

There is a world within you,
earth in your heart,
air in your lungs,
fire in your soul.

Picture every breath working
to make you whole.

The world places such emphasis on defining things. People want answers right away or to put labels on things that don't otherwise make sense to them. They want justification and instant gratification; they want things *now*, so much so that they can be too impatient to wait and see what may come or what may be. But the magic of life is not about definitions and labels; it's about love. About finding the beauty in the everyday motions of life. The next time you find yourself sitting in the front seat of your car, stop for a minute. Imagine the glass windshield as the universe. Now pay special attention to the tiniest speck of dust glistening in the sunlight. That speck is Earth. Where we live and breathe. How small we are compared with the vastness of the universe. But how important it is to live every day with purpose.

Here I was, and I was thinking about life
and how it can be demanding.

How there are just some days that feel worse
than others. That feel as though every moment
was made to make me feel less than I am.

What to do when
all the thoughts feel
all-consuming.

How do I go about my days when I
feel so out of place? When no matter how
hard I try, it seems far easier to hide?

And so, I thought of all the breaths I had taken
so far. Of all the steps I had already made.
Of all the memories I had woven, the dreams
I'd had, the hearts I had held.

And I continued
to think of these things
as I went about my day.

Because when the struggle feels like too much
and the day feels like I have swallowed the sun,
I remind myself of all the miles I have come
and the journey I have begun.

We surround ourselves with things that will help us understand the moments of darkness. Why in these moments it feels like our bodies have turned against us. Our chest is heavy, as though it has caved in, our breathing too quick and out of control. We look for the things that will explain this, tell us why we feel so exhausted from all the thoughts. But the explanation is buried deep inside of you. It's in the way you choose to rise again every morning, the way you hold your head high despite what anyone says, and mostly it's in the way you find the peace by taking deeper breaths.

On Tuesday, it was because the weather was too cold and you would have rather stayed in. On Thursday, it was because you had forgotten to turn the iron off and needed to run back to the house. On Friday, it was because you weren't sure what to wear, and by the time you had changed your outfit four times, the bar had closed. On Sunday, it was because the rain had come, and it was heavy, a rushing river blocking the driveway. And whether you believe me or not, I suppose it doesn't matter, but I will tell you anyway. Whether it's too cold or you don't know what to wear, whether it's the rain or your heart is in a lot of pain, I'd stay in with you.

There is a reason for you. The universe planted a soul, and from that tiny seed grew you. So, when you wonder if you should feel too much or embrace all that life can be, the answer is yes. You should laugh, and really laugh. You should cry and let the tears run free. You should dance in the rain, have honest conversations, breathe again and again. Live with all your intention, because the universe surely, wonderfully, truthfully intended that for you.

It was in the moment,
right as you leaned in
and you smiled against
my lips.

That was when I knew
you were magic.

That was when the world
opened up again
and everything that had
weighed me down
was suddenly released.

You will feel as though
you might be sad forever.

As though the anxiety
is impossible to breathe through.

You will feel as though life
was made to be out of control,
reckless with your heart,
unable to think rationally,
and all alone.

But you must remember
you are more in control
than you know.

And in the times it feels as
though even the simplest of tasks
are more difficult than
climbing mountains,
just remember to inhale,
hold it, and let go.

Be the reason someone
feels important and understood.

Be the reason someone smiles
when they see you and carries on
during all the difficult days.

Be the reason someone feels
joy and strength and that they
can breathe again.

There are some things you should do more of, like stop and watch the clouds go by. Release and let go. Follow butterflies. Laugh fully, completely, with your whole belly. Sit in the grass, out in the sun. Fill your space with the things you love. Inhale joy. All things to calm your heart.

Remind yourself of the things that bring you joy. That it is worth staying to watch another sunrise or another flower bloom. That it is worth staying for giant mugs of hot cocoa and warm scarves and whispering secrets to the stars and the moon. Remind yourself that there are people you haven't seen in a while who need one of your hugs, that you still have things to do, like dreaming and falling in love. Remind yourself that there is room in your heart for clarity and acceptance, and the negativity can leave. Remind yourself, life is about learning to stop every so often and breathe.

And with every small breath
you are sending a message
of hope to your soul;
you are saying,
we have today, tomorrow,
and forever to learn
what it means to grow.

There were days I believed I would not get out of bed. That I couldn't possibly make it through one day without you. That I would spend the rest of eternity hearing your voice in my dreams, your laugh down the empty corridor, your breath in the middle of the night. I wished I could have done something. Stopped the pain from creating holes in my heart, the same way asteroids create holes in the moon. But I couldn't stop the storm. I could only hope for the best when the dust had settled. And the dust did settle. One day, I stopped wanting to kiss you. I stopped wanting to hear your voice and feel your touch. I stopped wanting my days to revolve around you. And when that day came, the skies had cleared, the stars shone, and I knew I had finally managed to move on.

It was raining, the ground wet and water rushing from the pavement. Glasses left on the sink from all the nights I tried to fix this broken thinking. I let down my defenses, and now I'm losing sleep, always wide awake. Loving you only ever made me break. I'm left with all these issues from empty wishes. Just a throwaway love, waiting at a bus station for hope that will never come.

It was snowing, and I watched from the window as the frost made patterns across the ground. There were no more glasses, no more broken thinking. But I was searching for myself, reaching into the deepest parts of my soul, trying to remember who I was and who I wanted to be before you stole that from me.

It was warm, the sun was shining, and I was barefoot dancing under the sprinklers. And I was smiling. The front door wide open, the porch covered in potted plants, all regrowing, all renewing. And I was happy. Because I finally knew what it meant to be waiting at a bus station. Waiting for the driver to arrive, waiting to be free. Because the driver in my life had always been me.

There was a soul I once knew,
and even if her own hands shook,
she still held them out to others.

Even if her own heart ached,
she still opened it to the world.

Even if her voice trembled,
she still continued to speak up.

Even if there were days
she did not feel strong,
she still offered her shoulder
to lean on.

There are some people in this world
who show kindness in the way
the sky shows color—
bright, beautiful, and forever.

The hurt is not given to you
for no reason at all.
It is meant to be felt,
to be held, and to be released.

You honor yourself each time
you shed new skin,
breathe life into a new day,
by coming undone and
stitching yourself
back together again.

The anxiety gets caught between
the silence and the moonlight.
Turning over like the tide,
aching all night.

I know sometimes it feels like
you are made of glass,
like the smallest change
or challenge can feel crushing,
all-consuming, unimaginable.

But glass is also made from lightning,
and lightning brightens the entire sky.

Just like you.

Remember you are made
of light and wonder.
Remember your worth.
Remember that even in the darkness
you are still light.

I know that you feel as though something is always missing. As though your soul is scattered in a million tiny parts and you don't know which ones to pick up or where to start. After awhile, you start to wonder if any of these parts even belong, if you could undo everything you have learned about yourself and start again. But you do belong. Even if there are days you cannot cope. Even if there are days where nothing eases the pain. Always know that each day you are reinventing yourself. Each day, every single piece will be new. So, in the end, nothing can really be missing when every time the sun rises, you are renewing.

I just want to take
your hand in mine,
let you know that
everything
is going to be okay.

That even if you feel
scared, alone, uncertain—
there are still moments
to be had and
dreams to be lived.

There is a piece of my soul that will always be yours. Interwoven, locked, fused together with yours. Even through one hundred lifetimes, even if my heart belongs to someone else, that one piece of my soul is forever yours. It belongs to you because you are the person who reminded my soul to breathe.

For what seemed like a lifetime,
the days all blended into one.
I could not see the difference
in each day, and it clouded my mind.

For each and every new day
was different;
none remained the same color,
and none brought the same gifts.

So, when I began to see each new day
as its own story, it meant I could truly see,
and when I could truly see,
my soul could finally breathe.

mbrace the Silence

But how could I look at you
and tell you I didn't see the
sadness in your eyes?
How could I watch you as you
moved through your life
with your heart in pieces
and your soul on fire?

I wanted to take that pain
from you and carry it so that
you didn't have to.
Because I couldn't understand how
someone like you,
with so much light and so beautiful
in all that you do,
could be broken by someone
who didn't love you
in the way you deserved.

But it will make sense one day.

In the same way it didn't make
sense for me to carry your pain.
It was not my pain to carry.
It was yours.
This pain, your pain, brought into
your life to teach you that
you would survive.

That even though they
broke your heart

and they made you feel
like you weren't worthy enough,
or good enough, or beautiful enough,
it didn't mean that it was true.

Because I know you are worthy enough,
and good enough, and so beautiful.
I can't help but smile when I think of you.

Your journey doesn't always need to be about love. It doesn't always need to be about how you stitched yourself back together again after someone else broke your heart and went on to find someone new. Your journey can just be about you. About how you still moved forward in life but came to find hope in the empty sheets, forgotten sweaters, and quiet mornings. Your journey can be about the moment you realized you could depend on yourself. That life didn't always need to be chaotic or full of loud conversations. That life could be lived and fulfilling, even while alone. Life could be about your story and how you carry the same backpack with you everywhere, and dance in your living room, and eat cereal straight from the box. Life could be about your aspirations and connecting with your soul, thread by thread. Your journey can be about how you mended your heart and fell in love with yourself instead.

It was only when
she noticed the stillness
that she heard the beat
of the world.

It was only in the silence
did she become the wolf.

But fireflies exist in the darkness,
and stars and the moon too.
Such wonder and beauty covered
in the dark, shining in the silence.
It does not matter if you feel joy,
or pain, or sorrow; you can find
wonder in the silence and
all the wisdom for tomorrow.

My favorite moment
is the beginning
of every new day,
as the sky becomes lighter
and our alarms go off.

It's in those moments,
wrapped up in your arms,
that I could spend eternity in
those extra minutes of silence.

It is here that I feel
safe and loved.

You can feel everything in the silence. You can hear your heart drum in your ears, feel your breath as it moves throughout your body, smell the salt from the ocean in the air, taste the honey from the flowers blooming once more. In the silence you can reconnect with who you are at your core. You can find your spirit and promise to be braver and stronger than before.

We perceive a journey to be outside of ourselves, the road we travel, the path we walk, the quest we take. But the true journey is found when we realize that all the roads, paths, and quests are mapped within us. Our heart is our compass, our mind the wheel, our soul the sails. Once we understand that peace starts from within, then our true journey can begin.

The leaves do not stop moving,
even when the wind is soft;
a mere whisper, they still move,
much like our thoughts.

Our minds can be empty, or
our minds can be full,
and in both we are still worthy.

We should not resist
opening the door to the
quietest room in the house,
because even if this room
is filled with shadows,
it is still a part of our journey.

The shadows are something
we should embrace and nurture.

They should be something
we choose to love
so the light may return once more.

If you have only but a moment,
use that moment to let your feelings
unfold.

Listen to the truth
that awakens in the silence;
nurture the thoughts
that linger in your
mind.

Reach for the infinite possibility
of your goals and aspirations.

Find comfort in the silence and
inspiration in your mindfulness.

There were three different boxes, and inside one was anger, the other was pain, and the final was grief. And they lived in the attic of her mind, untouched, unfelt, closed. Until one day, as dawn fell upon her heart, she realized that to start the journey, she must first open the boxes. Because to feel anger, pain, and grief, as they are, in the moment they arrive, is to truly feel at peace with your mind.

I am learning to find answers somewhere in the silence, the time of day before the sun rises, when the birds awake and the moon disappears from the silky sky. I've been learning to listen to my heart, what it needs, the gentleness I should show, the forgiveness I need to learn and know. I've been learning to calm the dusty thoughts, let the silence become my strength, hold my hopes in the palm of my hand and feel their depth. I've been learning to continue my journey, brave and defiant. I have been learning to be at peace in all the quiet.

One day, there may be a moment
or a handful of moments strung together
when you desperately won't want to be here.

You will feel as though nothing matters
anymore, because each day is just too much.
There is no possibility of a silver lining.

And more than feeling this way, you will want
someone to prove you wrong. Someone to convince
you there is still a reason, or a handful of reasons.

So, this is why I'll remind you to stay.

Because if you stay despite the ache that you feel
and the deep pit of pain in your heart,
if you carry on despite all those days that feel
too much to handle, you will find those days thin.

You will find, sooner or later, these bright days return.
They will be small at first, slow, timid in their healing.
But they will come, to remind you of your worth and
all the good things you would miss if you did not stay.

And some more days after this, you will see how much
you have grown, how much you can be, and, most
importantly, how much of your life you still need to see.

The truth is most stories always begin with someone on the very cusp of being all they can be. Then a terrible thing happens, and their heart breaks a little more than it has before. So, this person, who is beautiful and worthy and deserves to be happy, is now lost, unsure, a little broken, and flawed. But what the ache can never take away is that this person deserves the chance to learn some more, be who they want to be, find out all the goals they can achieve and all the beauty they can see.

I just don't want to see
right through people,
I want to see them
for all the stardust
they are
and the capability
they have inside

I want to remind
them that
they have a story
that matters
and is worth
listening to

I want them to know
that their truth
is noticed and heard
in everything they do

There was once a time I swallowed words. I was too afraid to voice the things I really felt. As though the silence was all I was worthy of. But when I discovered that life is about layers, and that it will always have many layers, I realized that perhaps having a voice and embracing the silence can work together. That even in all the quiet, my thoughts matter, just as much as they matter when there is noise.

Somewhere in between the moment we met and the moment we left each other were thousands of moments of love. The first time we kissed, the first time I introduced you to my friends, the first time we shared all our secrets. So many moments, stitching my entire being into yours. Now I spend all these moments trying to remember what that felt like. Anything to drown out the ache and the silence of you not being here.

There is always that feeling
in the back of her mind,
to be very far away.

To be lost in the wilderness,
chasing landscapes as
beautiful as she.

To be climbing mountains
nobody would know,
finding hidden places no other
person would go.

To be lost when everyone
wants to be found,
to steer from the spotlight,
to go unnoticed,
surrounded by silence.

And then, one day,
I began to see
the good in listening and
the wonder in watching.

For every winding road,
a new adventure to have,
and for every forsaken path,
a new way to walk.

I found intimacy in the silence,
in understanding the delicacy
of each breath the earth takes.

And so now, I ask you:
do not look for me in the chaos
or in the broken thoughts
and the blinding, prolonged sadness.

I am no longer there.

Find me where the sun kisses
the horizon; love me
where the sky begins.

There was a lonely cottage across the way, and one evening, in the middle of a raging storm, a young girl made her way to the steps. She knocked three times, waited, and knocked three times more. Before long, a shadow greeted her and stepped aside, opening the door. In the foyer, the shadow introduced itself as Silence and with open arms told her not to be afraid, for it only wanted to talk. The shadow asked the girl why she so often thought such sad thoughts, why the quiet was all-consuming, unsettling, leaving her distraught. After a moment, the girl replied that in the quiet, she felt most alone; in the quiet, she could never seem to find her way home. In return, the shadow surprised her by being kind. In its hands it produced a light. The shadow told the girl to take this light and that when they parted, the light would sink deep within the girl's heart. For it is in the quiet that we each discover how important we are, how much we truly embody light.

She was learning to love herself the long way around. By waking up every morning with gratitude in her heart, even if some mornings it felt like the sun was barely shining. She was learning to love her books piled high in the corner of her room and her bracelets scattered across her windowsill. She was learning to love listening to the rain every time it stormed and the way she stirred her coffee three times before the first sip. She was learning that the birds singing in the afternoon and the sound of her wind chime calmed her in ways that steadied every beat of her heart. All the little, intricate things, from morning to night, were all the things that made her who she was. And in the process of learning to love these things, she learned to love herself.

vercome your Fear

It is easier to turn away from the things we don't understand, to give up on the things that cause us frustration and confusion. But it is in these things we find pieces of ourselves. Becoming equal, loving ourselves and each other, starts in finding familiarity in the things that make us afraid.

I learned to love
the most important parts of me,
because you did.

All my fear, anxieties,
quirks, and insecurities.

I overcame the struggle
because you held out
your hand and
offered to walk with me.

There is a space between where you have been, where you are now, and where you are headed. And in this space, you will become afraid. Afraid of all your past mistakes, afraid of every step you take today, and more so afraid of all the steps you will take every day after. But it is in this space that you can truly grow. For the fear is simply part of the journey, and to walk the road is to walk alongside the fear.

You are allowed to be afraid to fall in love with life. To fear excitement, adventure, making mistakes, weird things that bring you joy, and things that bring you pain. But you must take life in your hands anyway. For falling in love with life opens your heart to the greatest adventure you can live: finding yourself.

There were so many moments when she would begin to speak and then retract. When she would reach out her hand but pull away. As though there were an invisible thread, always holding her down, always stopping her from doing and saying the things she wanted to do and say. I wanted to remind her that she was capable of everything she wanted, that fear stopped her from living every day. But I knew she needed to learn this on her own. I knew that, despite all the twists and turns in the road, she would find her way back home.

It is because of fear that we choose to cling to the old memories rather than create new ones. It is within these old memories that we live, consumed with wanting to stay the same. For if nothing ever changes, perhaps we will always be safe. But this is not how life works. Change is constant, a forever river, an eternal sky. Our memories, our experiences, and our choices never stay the same. They are interwoven; old memories die and new ones are born. You can take an experience and let it ruin you, or you can take an experience, learn from it, let it become a second chance.

Butterflies see colors
that are invisible to us.

I imagine hope to be
like these colors.

While we cannot
often see it,
and even if
we are afraid,
hope still exists,
just like those colors.

We are afraid of the unknown; to step into a crowded room and bare your soul is like walking into a dark cave with no light and no way out. Your heart beats in a way that feels like you are an asteroid plummeting to the earth. You question your ability, your talent, and your very worth. Your mind spins like a record, and the number one song is "I Can't Do This."

But you can.

There is no other place for the fear and the anxiety to go other than with you and into the crowded room. If you feel them, come to know them, embrace them, then they are no longer a threat. Instead, they become a part of you, always with you but never defining you. So, you learn to carry them with you and walk into the room anyway.

We were standing in the space between now and tomorrow, just myself and all my doubts. We were quiet, not sure what to say, now that I had decided to say goodbye for a while. I wish I could have saved the moment, stored it away to always remember that the doubt was only ever there to drive me toward doing the things I never thought I was capable of doing. I have imagined how this moment would be. Played different versions over and over again. Sometimes I am still running, still afraid; other times I lie down, roll over, too exhausted to even try. But not today. Today, I am brave and fearless and all the things I know I can be. Today, I stand in front of all my fears, and I tell them that I am setting them free.

It was a gray sky kind of morning. She was in the corner of the room, watering her potted plants. She had a name for each one. She looked beautiful in the light streaming through the room. She had art that lined the walls, seashells scattered on every surface, a wind chime hanging right above her doorway. And I wanted to tell her that I was not afraid of her past. That the people she had loved before did not matter to me. That all her scars and her fears were now part of me too. But, instead, I watched her water the plants and hum the song she sang every time we tangled ourselves together in the sheets. I decided I would show her, for the rest of our lives, and I would do that by loving her for what she was and what she is and all that she can be.

The trouble was I looked for myself in the places that had already washed away. I looked for memories that were not my own. I searched the seas and skies for someone else's story instead of acknowledging that I already had a story, and it was built into all the tiny cobblestones of my driveway, the red painted door, the picture frames hanging in my home. I could not disown my struggles or my fears, because they would always return. They were mine. I had to learn to live with them, in the way I lived with choice and fate, and, more importantly, I had to learn that the journey does not have an expiration date.

There is a reason people speak of following your feet, listening to your heart, and trusting your intuition. It's because your soul has been here before; every journey, every road, is a magnet pulling you back home.

There are thousands of ways people tell you that you are beautiful, amazing, talented, and worthy. But all it takes is one person to tell you that you are less, that you don't matter, that you are not worth all the stars in the universe, and you unravel. Why is it that we pay more attention to the people who bring us undone than to the people who lift us up?

Think about all that you could do if you listened to all the people who wanted nothing but the best for you. The dreams you could live, the goals you could achieve, the kindness you could spread, and the way you could flourish instead.

So, if today someone has told you that your existence is a burden, that the thoughts in your mind and the things in your heart do not mean a thing, I am telling you to look here instead, because you mean more than the words people say. You mean the world, and the world is everything; you are magic on any given day.

She was everything I had ever wanted but everything I couldn't have. It was difficult; every time she looked at me, every touch, every kiss, every moment I wanted to tell the world I loved her, but I knew it was impossible. It was more than the need to tell people I loved her; it was about not losing her. If I lost her, where would I be? Every day, I hoped it would be different. Every night, I dreamt we would be happy together and not judged for who we were or whom we loved. I already loved her; she was my best friend. I was just trying not to be in love with her too. And it was this fear that brought the fairy tale to an end. The greatest mistake I have ever made was to give in to all the things that made me afraid.

If you want my advice, it is this: Don't write your story the way I did. Don't let fear control your narrative. Don't let fear destroy your happy ending.

There she was, staring out over a cliff, toward a sky filled with pink and lilac. So beautiful in all its colors, stitching all the memories of the day back together. And yet her heart ached for the unknown and yearned for what once was. Her eyes brimmed with tears as she fell deeper and deeper into the calls of her fears. "How can I love again?" she screamed to the valleys and the mountains and the ocean below. "How can I open my heart again to the things I have never known?"

And the waves of the ocean grew bigger, the valley turned to song, and the mountain stirred. Rising and emerging, the way the universe responds to a story desperate to be heard.

"You will love again, the same way the earth loves the rain. How it washes away the dread, how it breathes new life into the darkness and promises the rivers will be fed. You too will be nourished once more if you stop standing on the other side of a locked door."

It was as though, all my life,
I had been standing in front
of a wall.

And on the wall, I had hung
many pictures.

And each picture was
of something I feared.

And over time, I no longer
wanted to look at the wall.

The wall was neither comforting,
nor inviting, nor particularly
pleasant to look at.
But it was not the wall's fault.

For by not taking down
these pictures of fear,
I had not left any room
for the pictures that
belonged there,
pictures of my hopes and
my dreams and my successes.

And so, if we are unwilling
to remove the fear,
we lose ourselves in the
what-if instead of the what-is.

She was like the sun, the way she moved through life in a way that was effortless, strong, confident. She held on to moments so delicately, like the way light spills over valleys, yet she triumphed over every possibility the way day swallows the night. I was drawn to that, that pride in who she was, that unrelenting need to take back her power. I was just a shell of a person the first time I met her. Afraid of people, of moments, of truth, scared of the light I could be cast in.

One night, I sat across from her in the passenger seat of her car. Our song was on the radio, and she was looking at me, and I just knew she was the most beautiful person I would ever know. I loved the way she could laugh at nothing, the way she insisted on walking in the rain, how her bedroom was filled with old movies and old records, the way she would simply hold out her hand whenever I felt afraid. But that night, I didn't feel fear. I felt her light, and it washed over me in a way that promised I could be the sun too.

And when I leaned forward, she leaned forward too. Her lips felt like breathing fresh air. It felt like two people feeling after weeks of being numb. It felt like two people coming home to each other after months of being away. It felt like two people being found after years of being alone.

You choose not to love out of fear of heartbreak. You choose not to sing because what if you're off key. You choose not to travel because what if you get lost. You choose not to try something new because what if it isn't what you expected. And in the end, you've spent your whole life hesitating instead of living. Years from now, after all that is to be done and all my memories have been painted in the sky, I don't want to have arrived at the end knowing I was more afraid to live than I was to die.

It is always the things I cannot control that I fear the most. A plane falling from the sky, a runaway truck on the highway, a falling star Earth cannot defy, my heart breaking if you were to ever say goodbye. And in all these things that I hold on to, I turn them over and over again in my hands, wondering how to take control, how to hold on. But perhaps in all this wondering, I have been missing the key all along. Perhaps it is more in the way we accept that the fear will always be here. That our strength comes from walking side by side with what we are most afraid of. That just because we fear things does not mean we are broken. That life is about looking directly at fear and saying, "I know you are here, but you are not going to define this moment."

In the middle of winter, we were skating, around and around the ice rink. The snow was falling, and we were laughing. And while we hung to the side rails and tentatively put one foot in front of the other, a small child skated by, twisting, twirling, racing across the ice. She was fearless.

And so, I thought about childhood, the wonder, the ability to just leap.

When you are young, it is not about whether you will fall; it is just about taking the chance. Climbing trees and rocks with no ropes attached, riding bikes with no hands, being honest with no filter.

And I wanted to remind myself of this, in every moment I held back. I wanted to remind myself of the child within me, ready to take the leap, ready to see the world, as though I was always flying.

There I was, just a soul
away from my body.
Looking at the horizon,
and at the sun, as it slowly
began resting its weary head.

And as though she had heard me,
the moon began to rise above the
hill, the night all but setting in.
She had a face so milky white,
shaded with years of wisdom and
held up by so many
hopes and dreams.

The stars then followed, dancing
across the velvet sky,
daring me to join.
I so much wanted to float
toward them, but I was held back,
planted firmly to the ground.

For what if I did not dance like
the others and I did not shine as
beautiful as they?
For what if I was not smart
or strong like the rest and they
did not care for what I had to say?

But the moon simply smiled
and said, Child, you see the world
in a way I do not.

You are trapped by fear.
And when we are trapped by fear,
all that our soul can be vanishes
as we struggle to belong here.

But what can I do?

Live as the stars do.
Dance no matter who may be watching,
shine no matter the brightness of others.
Reach even when you feel like giving up.
Because to each star, the brightness of
its own light is always enough.

orgive your Mistakes

One day you are eighteen and the world tells you that you are too old to be making mistakes, yet you still feel too young to know how life really goes. You remember the way things were when you were small and how big the world seemed. The jungle gym felt like a castle and the sandpit an entire beach. Now you're a little older, and people expect you to be able to climb mountains without ropes. But lessons come and they go, and it won't matter if you are eighteen or thirty-three; the greatest lesson you can learn is that forgiving yourself is the way life should be.

There comes a point when you
need to stop being so angry at yourself.
You need to stop the anger from
eating away at your heart.
You need to acknowledge that what
you knew then is different from
what you know now
and what you will come to know.

It's about being honest. Honest with the people around you and especially honest with yourself. The things you can achieve and the happiness you find when you are honest with yourself are life changing. Suddenly, you stop wishing the weekend was already here, because every day feels special. You feel calmer, as life is no longer an enemy but rather a friend hoping the best for you. When you live moment to moment, you don't focus so much on the things you can't control; instead, you focus on how you respond to chaos.

There I was, but I was something else. A moth tucked away in my cocoon. Inside this safe space, I practiced forgiveness. I grew my heart ten times the size it should be, and I let all its love overflow onto me. I forgave everything I once was, ready to emerge as a better me.

Maybe not tomorrow or the time it takes for the earth to dance around the sun, but, someday, I want to know what it is to coexist with my mistakes. To know that I will not live a life free of them, but that this is okay. To exist alongside the mistakes but forgive them too, knowing they do not define me and all that I can achieve and do.

I hope you will stand in front of your mistakes and tell them that you will not let them dictate the way you live your life anymore. I hope you will find the courage to let them go. To acknowledge that you made the mistakes for a reason, but they are much like the leaves, falling and changing each season.

But you need to stop punishing yourself for all the things you did yesterday, or a month ago, or over the years that have long passed. You cannot unstitch these threads, and you cannot undo the paths they ran. But you can look to new horizons and accept a new sun. You can be kinder to a past you cannot outrun and more patient with a future that allows you to carry on.

The forgiveness is not a one-time thing. It happens over and over again. I am learning to forgive myself every time I spend an extra hour in bed, or on the days I leave all my texts on "read." I am learning to forgive myself in the times I choose myself over someone who needs me, because sometimes my well-being needs to come first. I am learning to forgive myself for not going to every party or event. I am learning to forgive myself on the days that are harder to be present. I am learning to forgive myself for missed opportunities or struggling with responsibilities. I am learning to forgive myself when I have lost my way, because being lost doesn't change who I am or how capable I am of seizing the day.

The more you learn to forgive yourself, the more you will learn to forgive others. This isn't to say that you forget the wrongs that have been done to you, but understanding the way someone else makes a mistake and needs forgiveness, just like you, helps to unite your heart with your mind and your soul too.

The forgiveness overlaps. You can be trying to forgive yourself for multiple things at once. But this is not the story of how a kingdom fell. It's the story of how one rose, and it rose to be a kingdom of hope, a kingdom that showed more empathy toward its heart. Because at the center of every kingdom is a heart that will continue to make mistakes, a heart that will continue to learn, a heart that is beautiful and bold and fearless, a heart that can grow only if it shows itself more forgiveness.

I was searching for myself
and I never meant
for you
to lose yourself
in the process too

I had given up on a love that could be kind or brave or unselfish. I was mourning a broken soul. I felt empty, helpless. But then I met you, and you changed so many of the everyday moments in my life. I could not go to sleep without calling you first; I could not go a day when I didn't think about the way you smiled or the way your hair curled around your face. How could I explain to anyone that you always smelled like honey or your voice knotted my stomach or that it didn't matter where we were—the cinema, the open road, the middle of the lounge room floor—if I was with you, I was home. I had always thought people were meant to bring you undone, and yet here you were putting me back together again.

The darkness deserves a home too. It deserves a safe space, blanket, cup of tea, and in that moment to just simply be. While you are blaming the darkness for causing all the ache, just remember that something as vulnerable as the shadows deserves to be nurtured despite all its mistakes.

It was the night I stumbled home from the bar and sat at the kitchen counter, the one that used to be ours. I pictured so vividly the months before; we used to cook dinner together. Now I barely eat, I barely sleep; I drown all the memories with vodka that tastes bittersweet. This home isn't even a home anymore. It feels like you weren't even here. All that's left is the grief from the night you disappeared.

That was the most difficult thing about loss: the way it insisted on being felt. The way my heart tried to refuse and my soul wished for answers that were no longer there. What would I be in the world without her? What would I do and where would I go? How would I live every beautiful moment if it was not her hand to hold and instead it was her hand I had to let go? If her eyes were not the first I saw in the morning light, if her laugh was not the only thing I heard above every noise? What would I do with my love for her if I could not lay it to rest? How would I forgive myself for not reminding her of my love more often before she left?

At my breaking point,
in my darkest hour,
I pictured my heart filled
with every name of every soul
in all the world.

I held them there, asked them
to forgive me, for while I carry
so many in my heart,
I have forgotten to carry myself.

You must remember that
forgiveness is courage
as it is strength.

You need courage to forgive
those who have hurt you
and strength to understand
your own grace.

It is through both things that
you learn worth.

You have worth the moment
you enter this world.

You are worthy of love,
adventure, joy, and forgiveness.

Just like the sun,
and how it travels
through the sky each
and every day,
from east to west,
the light takes a journey.

This is much like forgiveness.

You must rise every day,
and you must go through
the process.

The people around you
know the purpose you have.
They cherish the lessons
you are learning
and the beauty you hold
inside your heart.

It was raining when I heard: cloudy skies, windswept grounds, sadness in the air. I remember the day, not for what the world lost, because the world would never be the same without her, but for what I gained in my heart: perspective. How I could possibly gain perspective from a person I did not know is a strange story in itself. But still, I felt it, and you cannot deny a feeling that wants to be felt. Here she was, just like magic, with more life to live, and in a flash of a moment, she will no longer walk those steps. It reminds you that life is not fair. It reminds you that every day may be the last day you walk your own steps. Life is too short to hold on to anger, too precious not to forgive. Life is too important not to have every moment as though it's the last you will ever live.

There is an art to letting go of all the mistakes and failures, to paint with forgiveness rather than regret. But sometimes I do not know what to do with all these doubts and fears; I just know that I cannot carry them with me. They will only weigh me down, and such burdens that sit on my heart, they drown me while I try to swim, and they break my wings while I try to fly.

How to forgive yourself

By taking responsibility—

So, you hurt someone, or maybe they hurt you, and you haven't decided what to do with all the pain. But the only way for the river to run again is for the sky to open and let it rain.

By speaking the mistake
into the universe—

Let the universe bear witness that despite the mistake you have made, it does not change your place on this earth. Your healing begins when you speak of your journey to forgiveness and all its worth.

By making amends—

Forgiveness starts with an apology, sometimes to yourself, sometimes to others, always to your heart.

By not blaming yourself—

The blame isn't going to help you move on or learn to let go. Forgiving is about navigating away from all the guilt and learning of all the hope in the things that can be rebuilt.

By renewing—

Life always regrows from the dust and the ashes, and so too will you. There is more to this life than holding on to all the mistakes that in the end shouldn't ever control you.

You may feel small right now, as though the world is far too big and too many people are always one step ahead of you. But other people grow in their own way, and so should you. Lessons are learned at your own pace, victories are won by your own merit, retrospect is gained in your own time. You are not a failure just because some days are worse than others. You are not less just because you have scars. Instead of feeling small, look at all the space you have left to grow.

You will discover that it was never about making the mistake; it was in the learning that came afterward. The way you broke someone's heart and struggled with the guilt, how you said the wrong thing in an interview and the job went to someone else, how you left the car lights on and your battery died, how you forgot to call your friend when they needed you most and now you barely speak and you would give anything to go back and change that whole week. But you will see the power is in the lesson, the forgiveness is in the discovery, and the comfort is in the hope to do better. Because to learn from your mistakes and be gentle with your growth along the way is a step in becoming all you can be each and every day.

alue Solidarity

If I could look up
and talk to the Milky Way,
I would ask her
what I call this feeling,
when I feel everything
and everyone all at once.

What do I call feeling small
but infinite at the same time?

What do I call no longer
feeling alone and
instead part of something more?

We forget our togetherness when we step on others to get what we want. We forget who we are when we do not care whom we hurt to reach our goals. But if we learn to support each other in the way we wish to be supported ourselves, then there is so much more we can achieve in this world.

In the woods, beyond a forgotten house,
among overgrown wildflowers
and running creeks, lived an owl.

And one night, while the moon was full,
a firefly came to see the owl.

"I cannot change the world," said the firefly.

"What makes you say that?" asked the owl.

"Because I am but one tiny spark."

"Yes," said the owl, "but when you are together,
with all the fireflies in the woods,
the whole night shines."

At the center of the universe is a beating heart, the pulse of humanity. Beyond identities, labels, and beliefs is a profound sense of togetherness. It is within the walls of this heart that we can find our true selves, that we can create experiences that allow us to be our true selves. Beyond land, sea, sky, and stars is a rhythm to the universe, a wave of change and acceptance.

When I get to life's end, I am sure it will not be about just one memory but a collection of moments, stitched together like pieces of patchwork on a large and oddly shaped quilt. I hope that it will be filled with the people I have met and the places that have my heart. Like the summer I flew across the world to meet the person I thought I would love forever, but it was never meant to be. And, oh, how my heart broke. So, I traveled across the sea to an island that was jasmine and people who had very little, and my heart healed and understood the importance of love and gratitude. Or the storm one spring when the power went out and my mother lit candles all around the house and my father worried the curtains would set on fire. The winter in New York staying at the terrace with the brick walls and yellow rain boots by the door. The year I decided to live and let go and that I wasn't going to be afraid anymore. When I met you and loved you and married you in an old barn that we dressed up in fairy lights, and we danced the night away. I have to believe that the moments will be endless and haunting and beautiful, but they will be my moments, and I will love them equally.

The year I lost my grandfather, I visited his grave every Thursday afternoon.

There was an undertaker there, and I never said a word to him, except for one day, when the rain had come and the ground was soft and had started to sprout these tiny blue flowers all around the grave.

The undertaker had stopped, looked at the flowers, and said,

"Blue is my favorite color."

"Maybe he heard you," I replied. "I wish he were still here and we were together."

"We are together in death," the undertaker said. "We go back to the earth, and we become the land."

"But it is not the same."

"No," the undertaker replied. "That is perhaps the hardest part of the grief. Still feeling someone but not being able to touch."

And it made me wonder, about the people I love, if we should spend more time together while we are alive, more hugs, more I love yous, more walks hand in hand.

Sometimes it isn't so much about stitching yourself together but rather about unraveling all that you thought you were and all that you thought you knew—to find the core of what it truly means to be alive, to be human. The connectedness that runs in our veins, our purpose, our passion, our destiny. All the roads traveled or untraveled lead us back to what we were born to be: together.

You will always mean something to someone; there is always someone somewhere thinking of you. Someone looking for you in a room full of strangers, because your face is the one they call home. Someone is waiting to show you the picture they came across while scrolling on their phone, because they know it will make you laugh, and they love hearing your laugh. Someone is waiting for the summer, because they have a road trip planned to a festival far out in the middle of nowhere, but you're always the person to go nowhere with, because you make nowhere matter. Someone is dreaming of you, hoping for you, wondering how you are, because you are the bright spot in their day, the star. Someone is waiting to confide in you, because you never judge them for their secrets. Someone is waiting for you to return their call, because they miss you and haven't heard your voice in weeks. Someone is waiting on the stoop of their stairs, watching the city flurry by, hoping you'll show up soon, because there's no one better to watch the world go by with. Someday, you will thank everything that is ordinary in your life, because without all the beautiful, ordinary, everyday life things, well, it wouldn't be a life anymore.

I lifted my head to the trees,
noticed how their leaves were already
bloodred and orange.

They would soon fall
and return to the earth once more,
to become all but another memory.

But they would fall together,
and they would regrow together too.

But the days are fleeting,
even if I want them
to last forever and ever
for all of time—
so, I think that to exist well,
we must find meaning
within ourselves
and within each other.
Even if we struggle
and even if it's daunting,
we must exist together.

Possibility

As we move though each and every day,
and they are filled with joy or sorrow and
beautiful moments and moments of struggle,
we must look for the possibility in all things.

The possibility that one lyric will turn
into a meaningful song.

The possibility that a bed of weeds
will turn into a garden of flowers.

The possibility that a dream unfulfilled
will turn into many new dreams reached.

The possibility of becoming the breath
of fresh air someone needs in their day.

The possibility that your spirit will overcome
all the obstacles that come your way.

The possibility that together we can do more,
that united, we become so much better
than we were before.

There are some souls
always meant for you.
In every new moment
and memory, they will
always find you in
different ways.

The friend who picks up
all your pieces after your
heart breaks,
the neighbor who lends
you sugar when you
have none,
the teacher who told you
your dreams meant everything,
the stranger who hands you
an umbrella when the rain
begins to sing.

And in these moments
and memories,
with each act of humility,
you will be reminded—
even when times are dire,
you are surrounded
by those who care,
and feeling wanted and loved
will make the day a little brighter.

We broke each other in those last six months. We were in and out of love. When we were in, we were so in, and when we were out, it felt like the end of everything. When did our paths become so disconnected? When did our hearts cease to align? How did we arrive at the point where I was no longer yours and you were no longer mine? And we still don't know what life will mean in one or three or five years. But we do know that we needed space to find out who we both were when we were alone.

Late in the misty evening
I told you I wasn't leaving
That we'd stay awhile
Watch the sun come up together

I'm hoping you won't go
and leave me all alone
Because life without you
won't feel like life at all

I know you know
I know you know

When all the roads end
if it's you standing next to me
I'd do it all again

We poured the sun
into our hearts
and the moon into
our souls.
We aligned our minds
with the planets
and drew our laughter
from the stars—
together, we became
the universe.

We like to believe the butterflies will last forever and our hearts will always race every time the one we love walks into the room. And sometimes I still get butterflies when I see you, and my heart races when your car appears in the driveway. But more than butterflies and a racing heart, I feel security. It doesn't feel like a whirlwind and hoping you text back right away anymore. Instead, I just feel at ease every time you walk in the door. Like my home has returned, my person is back in my arms. And I never feel alone when I'm with you. I know I am loved. I know that I can do anything as long as I have you.

I consider the mind as I consider the sky,
open and vast and infinite.

Each day is lived in millions of different ways
and with millions of different thoughts.
But what brings me comfort in the night
is that there are some thoughts we will always
share in common.

> Thoughts that hurt us—
> *I am not good enough*
> *What if I lose everything*
> *Will anyone love me for me?*

> Thoughts that make us smile —
> clean sheets, a sunrise, hot chocolate,
> a fresh lawn, a long road trip,
> a song worthwhile.

And this is what makes me feel connected
to all the hopes we have and things we think.
How beautiful that the whole world is together,
as though we are never alone but forever in sync.

There were three different universes. In one, I had very little: a small home, just enough food, but a smile wider than the sky. In the other, I was in love, and it was beautiful, and we held on to our love and never said goodbye. And in the last, I struggled with demons in the night, yet I triumphed in the end, finding comfort in the light. But in all, I was always grateful, for with gratitude comes happiness, and happiness always finds us, either in togetherness or in solitude.

The road had gone on
for miles and miles.
Dusty, charred, unending.
Much like the pain I felt.
And I was exhausted.
So, I sat with my head
in my hands and I wept.
I wept for all the people
washed away from my life.
I wept for all the trouble
that had come my way.
I wept for the hope
that seemed so far away.

And as though the universe
had heard my tears,
the sky broke open with rain,
and in every droplet of water
a message was delivered—

To hurt isn't to lose.
Feeling pain does not
make you weak.
It is what we do with pain
and the path we choose
that eventually brings us back
from the brink.

With the rain washing over me,
I finally allowed myself to see
that, even on this dark road,
I had never been alone.
Because the universe had always
been right beside me.

Speaking of beautiful things,
might you pause a moment
in time and listen to the sound
of laughter when the sun returns—
how even strangers look at
each other with a hint of joy
in their eyes

You can give pieces of your heart away, to friends and soul mates and lovers. You can give pieces of your soul away, to new adventures and cities and bright colors. But you must remember you. Remember your beautiful heart and your brilliant soul. Remember the light in your body and the wonder of your smile. Open your eyes; look at yourself once in a while.

This is my hope for you:
that you find purpose
in every path you walk.

That you live a life filled
with laughter
and the things you love.

That you see beauty
in the small details
and find comfort
in the arms of someone
who truly cares for you.

That your friendships
make you feel like you belong,
that the world shows you kindness
and compassion on the roads
that are dark and long.

And my greatest hope
is that you know courage
and patience forever,
that you know the world
is always a little bit brighter
when we stand together.

ractice Patience
& Gratitude

There are always
different stories,
different paths,
different perceptions.

Just because you see
something one way
does not mean the person
you love sees it the same.

This is what it means
to be patient and understanding.

When you can walk through
life side by side,
not one in front of the other.

You will apologize more often
than not because you are afraid
you have done something wrong.

You will constantly think of yourself
as being a burden or annoying
or embarrassing or the last person
anyone would want to spend time with.

You will struggle to be comfortable,
and too much of seeing people
will wear you down.

You will often not reply,
because things will feel out of control
and little things bring panic.

But here is my promise to you:

Every time you apologize,
I will say everything is okay.

All the moments we spend together,
I will remind you they're all my favorite.
When you feel uncomfortable,
we can leave,
and there isn't any need to reply,
as long as you know I'm always here.

As long as you know I'll always keep trying,
as long as you know your anxiety
doesn't mean I love you any less.

As long as you know I'll always be patient,
that for eternity
I'll put you before the rest.

All that you are will demand
your patience, understanding, and resilience.
You will be tested at every crossroad,
with every breath and every leap,
but to know life for all its worth
is to climb every mountain,
no matter how steep.

On some days,
it is important
to fall in love
with the colors
in a sunset
and on others
with a smile
from someone
who lights up
your life.

But on most days,
it's important
to fall in love
with yourself.

Even if you
cannot find
strength,
even if you
feel a little lost,
love yourself
anyway.

August had been a difficult month. Heart had been broken, left to pick up the pieces when Love walked away. And, oh, how Heart had wept. Not knowing why Love had even left. And Mind struggled too, for it had always known what Heart had not. And so, on went the months, and Mind and Heart drifted apart.

Heart left where it had fallen, and Mind moved forward.

One day, Mind asked Heart to meet just beyond the hills, where the sun shone most. A beautiful lake, with a farmhouse nearby, to watch all the trees and the geese fly by.

"Let us meet here," Mind said to Heart. "Somewhere peaceful, somewhere we can be together again."

Heart agreed, and they decided on a time.

So, Mind waited at the meeting point for Heart. Seconds turned to minutes and then minutes turned to hours, but Mind remained patient, knowing sometimes it just took Heart a little longer to see what Mind already knew.

That for all the shadows in the world, there are many more stars. That for every break and scar, there is much more healing to be done and many more journeys in determining who you really are.

Eventually, Mind spotted Heart, walking across the fields, the sunlight dancing all around in small but magical swirls. And Heart sighed a deep breath when reaching Mind, for finally closure had been found.

"Thank you," Heart said, sitting down beside Mind. "I am sorry it took me so long."

Mind put an arm around Heart and smiled. "Oh, Heart," Mind said, "I knew you would make it."

There is no shame in being young. You do not need to be afraid of your feelings. If the walls come down around you, it is okay. Life always changes. It will not be as it is today, tomorrow, or the next day or a year from now. You change, and so does life. There are times you run in parallels, and other times you intersect, and sometimes you couldn't be further apart. But it is important to take the moments as they come. Wherever you are right now, or whatever it is that brings you joy, embrace that. Just be young.

Your body has always
been patient with you
Patient as you whispered
all the things you would
change in a heartbeat
Patient every time you
looked away from the mirror
Patient when you cursed yourself
for eating something sweet
Patient when you laughed
and called it such unkind things

But it should be you
who is patient with your body
To know it will change
time and time again
To understand every
stretch, mark, and scar
is what makes you beautiful
exactly as you are

It was always the long, drawn-out days,
the ones that blurred well into the night
and into the new morning again and again,
how you couldn't get out of bed, or shower,
or return any of my calls.

And I would miss you, terribly.
I would wonder when I would see you—
for coffee, or just to sit on the beach,
staring out at the ocean.

We used to listen for the stories,
as they washed up on the sand with every new tide.
You would smile and say,

> *"Can you hear the ocean whisper?*
> *She is calling out our dreams."*

But days went by and then months, and I began
to wonder if we would ever hear the stories of the ocean
once more and taste the salty air in between our lips,
as they danced over each other, always gentle,
always wanting just a little bit more than before.

Until one hour in the early dawn, you called.
"Have you forgotten me?" you asked.
"I could never."

And when we see the ocean once more, I am sure
she will tell you the most beautiful story of all—
sometimes the patience lives in the

understanding

You remember what heartbreak feels like even years later, even after all has healed or new love has flourished. You'll remember your heart stopping and then breaking and the silence that followed. And for a moment, a split second, a fraction suspended in time, you will remember that love, the one that broke you in two, and you will remember the journey that came after, like a ghost, revisiting old memories. You will remember the way you fell apart, slowly, then all at once, how long it took to stop crying over their name or wanting to text them during the day. But you will also remember the changing, the stitching yourself back together. You will remember how patient your mind was with your heart; you will remember all you have learned. That after heartbreak, we are never the same, but life continues on, once the sun has returned.

And then I heard her
whisper through the dark,
"Be patient with me,
for I cannot make sense
of all this mess in my heart."

How I just wish you love,
above all other things.
That safeness and warmth.
That joy in another's laugh.
That excited, racing heart.
That hand you can't let go of.
How I wish for this someone
to arrive at your door.
Remind you how beautiful you are.
That you deserve the world and more.
And as patience proves, my friend,
that someone will come along
and make you feel love again.

When I returned home,
after months away,
all the plants in my garden
had withered.

There was nothing left,
only the soil.

So, I took my watering can
and began to water every pot.
I placed them in the sun
and made a wish on a blue
robin that flew by.

And slowly, they began to regrow.
For even if I could not see,
it had remained true that the roots
were still in the soil.

You can return once more too.
Beneath the surface of your skin
and under the worries of today,
you still have your heart and soul.
You still have your story.
All you need is a little patience
and a little love to regrow.

I was always out looking for love, in all the places I thought it may be, and every time love did not appear, I was disappointed. For why did love not want me, when I had a heart so willing to share? Until in time, as it happened, I decided to let love go. I decided to live life for me. I would do the things I dreamt of doing, I would laugh with my whole being, I would find joy in the things worth seeing, I would spend moments in interesting places and find spaces filled with light, and I would teach my heart it's always best to be a little warmer. And in doing so, love found me one day, unexpectedly, as I walked around a corner.

I have watched on as she explained that she is not an easy person to love. That some days are harder than others. That on the good days she will not be able to keep her hands away, or her lips from my lips, or her eyes from undressing all the parts of me. But on the bad days, she will curl under the covers, unable to move or to speak, if only to whisper quietly.

I have listened as she explained the long and winding road she has been on all these years. How in the moments she is cold and distant, she is ashamed, fearful I am unable to recognize the person I fell in love with. How sorry she is that not every moment can be light, that the heaviness gets in the way.

And always in these moments, no matter how many times she forgets, it is important for me to say that I will love her every morning, no matter tears or a smile, that I will love her in every struggle, every bad thought, every fight. As much as I will love her in every success, every beautiful moment, all day and all night.

Every time she says that she is not easy to love, I tell her that love itself was never made to be easy. Every time she wonders if the way I love her will ever change, I tell her that everything I have to offer her is wrapped up all inside of me, that I love her as though I have swallowed the universe and all its entirety.

I will always be grateful for her laugh and hand-holding and her eyes lighting up when I tell her how much I love her. And kissing, I will always be grateful for kissing. Especially that slow, half-asleep kiss, when you take her with you into your dreams.

The Swing

On a warm fall day, I greeted Life in my front yard.

Spread out across the lawn was a pile of different things. Some timber, some rope, some nails and tools. And I asked Life, "What are you doing?" and Life told me, "I am building you a swing."

Excited, I rushed over and began to pick up various things. "Wait," Life instructed, "let us take our time."

So, bit by bit, Life began to construct the swing. Back and forth with the tools, hammering away at the timber, carefully threading the rope. And moments went by, one long, drawn-out hour after the next. "Surely it does not take this long to build a swing!" I said, and I sat down with a sigh.

But Life continued building the swing, slowly, putting each piece together with care. Until finally it was finished. And moving aside, Life offered me a hand. "Here," said Life, "you take the first ride."

So, on the swing I went, and Life gave me a nudge, and up into the air I rose, with the wind in my hair and the sunshine on my nose.

"I feel like a bird," I called, as I reveled in all the clouds dancing across the sky.

"Yes," smiled Life, "for if we are not patient, then we will not be able to fly."

I have always loved
the way you have
just lived.

The way tiny details
bring you such joy.

That despite what
anyone says,
you forge ahead anyway.

The way you are always
so patient with me,
willing to learn,
wanting to ride
every wave together.

Of course, this is how
I know I love you;
for your love,
I'd wait forever.

You survive by always being honest. Even when the truth hurts, it is still the truth, and the truth must always be said. You survive by offering your hand to someone who cannot get up. You survive by offering your smile to someone in tears. You survive by never measuring yourself against others. You survive by choosing joy over rage. You survive by taking time to know yourself the way you know your favorite book. You survive by loving every part of you: your soul, your mind, the way you look. You survive by refusing to let mistakes rip you apart. You survive by waking up each morning with gratitude in your heart.

You can spend your whole life relearning the same things more than once. And this is what I believe magic is. There is always inspiration found from the story, no matter how many times it is written. There is always a lesson to be found, no matter how many times you read the words. The conversation can be had again and again, and all the while, you can find yourself a thousand new times.

Some of the most important lessons I have learned in my life are all connected to patience. To be patient when I make mistakes and patient when I say the wrong thing. To be patient with love and how it means many things and is disguised in many different ways. That sometimes true patience is understanding not everyone has the same heart as I do, but it doesn't mean I need to give them any less of my heart; you never know when you'll change someone's course for the better. And perhaps the most important lesson is that I cannot expect someone to give all of themselves to me, because a piece must always be reserved for just them. For when we leave just one piece entirely and completely to ourselves, we learn what being patient really means.

Promise me this: That you will always remember time is fluid. That nothing is the end of the world. That even if you feel the walls caving in, there is still the option to move. You will always have the choice to start again. That no matter how many doors close, there will always be one that opens. So long as your heart is patient and your mind is clear, you will find what you are looking for, and you will be happy in all that you hold dear.

We find gratitude in caring for the things we love, like watering a potted plant upon our windowsill or cooking a meal we have chosen for our family or running our hands up and down the arm of the person we love. We find gratitude in a dotted starry night, or snowcapped mountains, or an ocean as blue as blue can be. We find gratitude in our favorite songs and art and poetry. When we fill ourselves with the things we are grateful for, our hearts overflow, and when our hearts overflow, life becomes more beautiful than we have ever known.

We beep before the light is green and can't wait our turn for more than one minute or fifteen. We become frustrated with others simply trying to learn, even if it's a new job or an impossible turn. We grow impatient when the elderly are crossing the street. We can't wait more than five minutes in a drive-through and become frustrated with waitstaff when we go out to eat. We look at a long line and refuse to join or become annoyed at the grocery store with someone counting out their coin. We rush from one moment to the next and seemingly will life away. Sometimes it feels like we complain in every moment of every day. And if only we stopped for just a moment in time to realize all that we have and all we can be, that patience is important for both you and me. To know life's true beauty is to surely understand that everyone in life is just doing the best they can.

hoose Kindness

I have been learning to open my soul. Every day, as the sun rises, I remind myself to give a little more. To smile at a stranger while out for a walk, let the mother with a crying child take my spot in line, hold open the door, give up my seat on the train, ask someone how their day is, offer an umbrella in the rain. I have been trying to encourage positivity and trying less to complain. I have been trying to be a light when another is in pain or afraid. I have been thinking about compassion, how it is more beautiful than the brightest colors in the sky. I have been thinking about how kindness first starts within myself and all the days that I continue to try.

To show your soul
is to give your time,
to listen, to be fully
and completely
present in the moment.

Even in the moments
it all feels like too much,
and your heart is heavy
and your soul weary,
you can still be kind.

Even in the darkest moments
of your life,
kindness is the greatest light
that shines.

And if there were a story she wanted to share more than all the others, it was the story of how she found herself in a forgotten town, where the people had very little but were happy. A town with so few riches yet so many smiling faces. A town with so many of their own stories, in every pocket, corner, and tiny space. She wanted to tell the story of a community that she would remember with fondness. A community that taught her spreading kindness creates more kindness.

There will be a time in your life, and it will be the most difficult set of moments you will ever go through. You will feel challenged at every road, burdened as though you are not enough. You will wonder if closing yourself off to the world is better than remaining soft. Some days, the anxiety will want to swallow you whole, and the desperation you feel will be the greatest desperation you will ever know. You will wonder if you are worth the struggle, if your kindness and compassion to others hold any value if they are not returned to you too. But there are lessons to be learned in the power of giving rather than taking. Because in your darkest moments, the kindness you show to your own heart is the very thing that will allow the healing to start.

More than learning about your favorite color,
or how you have your coffee, or the clothes
you choose to wear, I want to know how
kind you can be.

I want to know the way you treat your waiter,
the way you look for a person's soul rather
than their mistakes, the way you respond
to anger or pain, the way you choose
compassion rather than what you can gain.

It was after a trying month, with many ups and downs, sleepless nights, and too many times I had shed rivers of tears. I had been coming home in the early evening, tired from a day that had been filled with struggle. A woman had stopped me, asked which way to the train. I had pointed and replied, "It's only down the lane." She had smiled with a smile that could have filled all the dark corners of the earth and replied, "You have beautiful eyes." And I watched her go, disappear into the fading light of the day, and how the warmth spread from ear to ear in a smile that had taken me all month to feel. A light at the end of a dark highway, magic at the end of a mile, and all it took was one simple moment of kindness to return my smile.

You cannot always
choose to the be bravest,
wisest, or strongest.

But you can always
choose to be the kindest.

You deserve a love that won't shame you for being who you are, that will rise with you, encourage you, dare you to dream and seek. You deserve a love that strengthens you when you are weak, that reminds you of all the joy you bring to the universe, that even just the mention of you makes their heart explode like fireworks.

Her existence was so delicate,
so soft in the way she walked
through the world.

I just wanted to remind her to
keep her heart grounded
and honest and true.

To keep spreading kindness
in all the things
she ever set out to do.

I have been trying to be less selfish and more giving. I have been trying to be less impatient and more patient. I have been trying to be more present and less absent. I have been trying to be more focused and less unfocused. I have been trying to be kinder to my heart and less punishing. I have been trying to learn that sometimes less ends up being more.

Things happen and they aren't supposed to, like snowfall in the middle of summer, red wine spilling on carpets, and birds flying north instead of south for the winter. So, when they break your heart, and you don't feel as though kindness is supposed to be the response, just know that being kind, even if people were not kind to you, always makes for a better you.

There have been many moments my heart has been touched. Through letters and songs, adventures and the open road. Through sunsets lighting the sky in all kinds of colors, through shooting stars and important conversations. Through stories, compassion, kindness, and the wild. But mostly, my heart has been touched by someone far more enchanting than any view—that person being you.

In all the chaos,
the constant is always love.

In all the fear,
the constant is always kindness.

In all the uncertainty,
the constant is always humility.

The year had been long
filled with doubt and pain
and hope had been dashed
for normal life to begin again

The days grew weary
as though giving was no
longer a gift
but rather a trade for
something in return
As though putting others
before yourself
was no longer taught
and no longer learned

And filled with this despair
I found myself deep
within the woods
looking for an answer
Some semblance of life
to give me a reason to go on

I stumbled upon a bank
of overgrown leaves
and behind the leaves
was an old willow tree

"Tell me of hope once more"
I said with tears in my eyes
"Tell me how to live in a world
with such cruelty and lies"

And the willow tree said—
There will always be darkness
in the world and shadows
that lurk on every path
But this does not mean
life succumbs to such a wrath

Fill your lungs with laughter
and your heart with dreams
Fill your soul with compassion
and allow your mind to believe

For more than this darkness
that consumes so much space
exists the light of love
to remind us of such grace

In the human body, it has been said that cells are regrown every seven years. And so, I wonder about the soul and how many times we can regrow our soul. Does it carry memories from every life, would I know my soul in every new body, would I know the other souls I have met along the way? And if to regrow is to start again, then I want to take the important things along with me. Goodness, honesty, love, and gratitude.

Fields of lavender sprawled
as far as the eye could see
Each flower bursting with color
And oh!
How they sang and called to me
Each call a message of unity

For each flower
came together in color
to spread across fields in beauty

Much like the way people
should work together
to achieve kindness and humility

Even if I do not know your story
       and I have never lived in your shoes
       I want to listen to your hopes
       and all the dreams you choose

Tell me what breaks your heart in two
       let me hold your hand so together
       we can walk through the shadows

Through every valley and every tunnel
Through every mountain and pile of rubble

For, walking with you, I will surely start to see
       what it means for compassion to
       fill every part of me

For, tomorrow, when the sun rises once more
       I hope to be a little kinder
       than I was the day before

Faith is something that rises
from the dust and ashes
And it wraps around us silently
and whispers to trust its course

And it is the warmest hand
and the dizziest feeling
When we feel such hope
from our smile to our toes
It heals all the aching our
soul has known

So, when you show compassion
you also instill faith
in those who have lost it all
And it is this empathy you give
without expecting anything in return
that is the greatest gift of all

If I can bring light to one broken soul
   then I will have lived
If I can place myself in another's shoes
and imagine their plight
   then I will know what empathy means
For to know another's journey
and show compassion with certainty
is to see a person in their entirety

Here is the world, and it can be daunting and frightening and haunting. But it can also be magical and enchanting and beautiful.

I've been thinking about how people hold open doors and elevators, and how they hand you the checkout divider when you are next in line. I've been thinking about how people help mothers with their strollers up the stairs, and how sometimes we sit next to strangers on roller coasters at county fairs and we laugh and we look at each other like we've known each other for so long when really we are just enjoying a moment in life together and it doesn't matter who we are or where we have come from.

I've been thinking about when someone smiles or their laughter fills the room and, even if you don't know them, it can be as joyful as springtime when flowers bloom. I've been thinking about the bus driver on my daily route, how he always asks how my mom is and says to have a good day and I don't know what I would do if it wasn't the first thing I heard him say. I've been thinking about the woman who walks her dog at the same time every afternoon, and we pass each other by, and she gives a little wave as she carries on her way.

I've been thinking about when people fall, there are hands that reach for them right away, and when disaster strikes, people always ask, "How can I help? What can I do today?" I've been thinking more about the way people are kind, because when the world is struggling and not coping the way it should, more often than not people choose to be good.

ind your Light

When you begin to learn things about someone, like the scent of their skin or the rhythm of their heartbeat or the way they eat their cereal in the morning, suddenly everything that doesn't hold true value begins to disappear. Suddenly it doesn't matter about the scars they keep or the burdens they carry; it's more about finding resource in their energy. Everything comes down to the light that they are and not just the light that you can see.

It's not always about what you want to hear but what you need to hear. If you listen, I would tell you about the light that spills from your eyes every time you laugh. I would tell you scars are merely memories woven into your skin. I would tell you the struggle shapes the person you will become. I would tell you the sorrow that you carry has only made you stronger and the battles that you face don't have to be faced alone.

There are dreams that exist in the spaces
between the words "I love you,"
and those dreams are filled with light and strength.

Know that whenever you enter a room,
your smile lights up every space.

Know that you deserve to love who you love
and always feel safe.

Know that who you are will never be a burden,
even if there are parts of the universe still learning.

Know that you will always belong here,
to live a life without fear, that you deserve hope
and happiness and good health.

Know that today, tomorrow, and forever
you should always be yourself.

For every branch that falls along the forest road, there is a light waiting in the shadows clearing the path for a person it has not even met. This light goes about its day, making others feel at home. A light that always reminds you that you are never alone.

I had always viewed her light and spirit as one. She was wild and soft, kind and thoughtful. She was the type of person who would show up at your door in the middle of the night and insist on swimming in the moonlight. She was the type of person to cross a room full of crowded people and kiss you as hard as she could. I knew that life with her would be an adventure, a never-ending story. She was the sunshine you long for after months of rain, the shoreline you return to every late evening to watch the sunset again and again. She was the type of person who made days dizzy and all a blur, and she meant so much that my heart just couldn't stop talking about her.

There was nothing about you
that was ever wrong in the first place.
You were not made in error;
there is no mistaking that everything
you are was intended.
The night loves all of the moon
and her many phases.

Life has been here, as old as the trees and mountains, as far and as wide as the rivers and the sea. And all that you are and how you exist is wrapped into the beautiful, intricate details of this earth. All the dusty roads and the colors painted in the sky, as beautiful and needed as every hello and every goodbye. When you walk these long roads to find the place you can call home, remember it is not about the distance but the passion in every step; it is not about the time it takes but rather your patience in finding yourself and forgiving your mistakes.

If I was to rearrange the universe,
you would be the sun,
because there is no other light
that warms me quite like you.

And people will ask
what happened to you
in the deepest and darkest
parts of the night
And you will reply softly
maybe barely at all
"I was searching for the light"

On a warm day, after the rain had come and gone,
I sat on my balcony, watching the birds in the trees
until the wind rustled and they flew upward—
spiraling, scattering, separating, and flying away
And perhaps this is what life really is
You move forward in all sorts of directions,
but you do fly, and you carry on anyway

I know what it is like to feel lost and apart from myself. To look at my life in front of me and think about what it may become and if only it would hurry and skip all the parts that will hurt. I know what it is like to lose people and dreams and hopes, to feel stuck and as though life is moving backward, not forward. I know what it feels like to feel empty when the rest of the world feels full. But every day that is given to you is a gift; sometimes it is just in the way the sheets feel after they have been washed, or a cup of coffee that feels like the best cup you have ever had, or the way the sun pokes through the clouds like spotlights lighting up a stage. Sometimes it is friends texting you goodnight, or a call from someone you haven't spoken to in a while, just wanting to check in. Sometimes it is the calmness of your heart after you realize a bad day is just a bad day, and it doesn't measure your purpose or how much you are a work of art.

Things I've come to know, and you will too

You will sabotage your own happiness because you're afraid to lose it, but it's in these moments that you're spiraling out of control you'll find what helps you endure life's greatest challenges.

You deserve love and affection and to be treated as though you are the brightest light in the universe.

To value yourself is to value what you do with your time. As you grow older, time becomes the one thing you cannot get back. Choosing what you want to do with your time is realizing your time is just as valuable as anyone else's.

Self-doubt holds you back in ways unimaginable. It prevents you from achieving all the things you are capable of achieving.

The things that bring you joy are the things that get you through each day. Hold them tightly in your heart and never let go.

Worrying about what others think or comparing your journey with theirs is as productive as driving with the hand brake on.

Not everyone will like or want to hear your story, but it doesn't make it any less valid or important. You will always have purpose, and your story will always be enough for you.

Sometimes the world feels like too much, like a beating pulse that rises and falls. We see so much pain and people broken, and we wonder where humility has gone, if we'll ever be truly rid of greed and entitlement, if people will choose light rather than hatred. But I spend every day waking up thankful, thinking about you and knowing we can get through it all together, like we always do.

When bad things happen, you turn into what others need you to be. Suddenly, you are the light at the end of all their turmoil. You are the strength they need, the comfort they want, the relief they crave. In all of this, it is important to stop for a moment. Understand that it is okay to feel overwhelmed, to feel afraid, to not know how things are going to end up. Because in between the moments of uncertainty and certainty, there is a space of becoming. There is the road you decided to take and the road you decided to leave behind. There is a string that connects your heart from who it wanted to be and who it will ultimately be. There is a lifeline to reach for, hold on to, and breathe in, and that lifeline has always been—and will always be —hope.

Leave room in your heart
for the people who will surprise you.

The people whom the world gives up on.

Those are the souls who need
the most forgiveness, the most encouraging,
the most room in your heart.

If there is something that you look for each and every day, look for hope. You will find it in a smile from your best friend, a wave from your neighbor, books you cannot put down, warm mugs of tea, a hug from someone you love, your favorite artist or song. You will find it in every corner, every pocket. Even if sometimes it feels as though hope is not there and you cannot see, hear, or feel it, know that as constant as the sun sets and rises, so too is hope on the horizon.

A butterfly takes time. It does not emerge without transformation, without process. Every stage is unique and individual; every stage matters so that the final metamorphosis is beautiful. You are like this too. You need time, you need courage, you need reflection.

I remember when I used to crawl
into bed at the end of every day
with a heavy heart.

I remember when I used to second-guess
myself and question every thought,
every action, every dream.

I remember when I could not
find the joy in any of the things
I loved, even if I desperately tried.

I remember when I couldn't watch
a movie or eat a bowl of cereal
without crying.

I remember when the sadness filled
every day the same way
it filled every night.

But my memory isn't as raw
as it once was; there is time in between,
there is healing.

And even if those memories
will always be in my past,
I know that they do not define my future.

In the search for all the worth I knew I had within, I needed to understand that it would not appear all at once. I needed to realize that being whole was about many different, smaller parts in between. And it would take all these parts to build a home. A staircase is not a staircase without the first step, a fireplace is not a fireplace without the first brick, a roof is not a roof without the first tile.

Just like a heart is not a heart without a beat, a smile is not a smile without warmth, a soul is not a soul without light. Each and every part, working together to remind me that I would make it through every dark night.

I decided to take Recovery on a date. During this date, we talked about all the ways we would need each other, all the ways we would lose each other, and all the days we would find each other again. We shared a chocolate sundae with extra strawberries, and I told Recovery she looked good. She said I looked good too; I just couldn't see it in the way she could. I told Recovery I had spent the last year afraid of myself and what I might do and that I needed someone to hold my hand, remind me of the things my mind tried to forget but my heart always knew. Recovery promised to hold my hand, even though I still had a long way to go, a gentle reminder that, despite everything, we could still fit together. It was only then did I realize my strength could make us work forever.

In time I hope you understand—
You don't need to be
the entire sky or the highest mountain,
the tallest tree or the whole ocean.

You are a flash of color
within a beautiful sunrise,
a snowcapped peak,
the crown upon the mountainside.
You are the roots beneath the tree,
an ancient foundation born in the night,
a drop in the sea, forever and always
glistening in the moonlight.

When you expect too much of yourself,
you lose the magic of what it means
to simply and truthfully just be you.

It's not always going to be bubble baths and face masks. It's not going to be waking up in the morning and suddenly you are changed, a new person, better than you have ever been before. Healing isn't a straight line; it's an entire notebook of scribbled ink. It's blotchy, angry, messy, filled with ripped pages. It's convincing yourself to open the windows; it's arguing with yourself to drink water, to eat, to sleep enough hours and not any more or any less. Healing is leaning on people, even though your pride gets in the way. It's calling your therapist, making an appointment, going, and making another one. It's holding your mind, heart, and soul at arm's length and reasoning with them to come together, to get on the same page for once. It's finding the meaning in poetry, books, meditation, and gratitude, even when those things felt meaningless to you before. It's promising yourself you are going to continue to take better care of your own needs, even if it is a constant battle. It's reminding the universe and yourself that you want to exist, you want to be here.

The same day
you plant a seed
is not the same day
you will see the tree
or the forest rise
before you.

It will take years.

But when you
nurture the seed,
pour your heart into it,
water the foundation,
award sunlight,
patiently watch it grow,
the forest will prosper,
and it will become home
to many more
beautiful things.

If you treat your soul
the same as a seed,
then over time, slowly,
your soul will become
home to many beautiful
things too.

Thank you for reading this book.

I hope you enjoyed reading it as much as I enjoyed writing it.
You can view more of my work on Instagram
@courtneypeppernell or TikTok @courtneypeppernell.

Feel free to write to me via courtney@pepperbooks.org.

Pillow Thoughts app now available on iOS
and Android stores, worldwide and on all
devices—download yours today!

Andrews McMeel Publishing
a division of Andrews McMeel Universal
1130 Walnut Street, Kansas City, Missouri 64106

www.andrewsmcmeel.com

21 22 23 24 25 BVG 10 9 8 7 6 5 4 3 2 1

ISBN: 978-1-5248-6751-5

Library of Congress Control Number: 2021936769

Editor: Patty Rice
Art Director/Designer: Diane Marsh
Production Editor: Elizabeth A. Garcia
Production Manager: Cliff Koehler

Illustrations by Justin Estcourt

ATTENTION: SCHOOLS AND BUSINESSES
Andrews McMeel books are available at quantity discounts with bulk purchase for educational, business, or sales promotional use. For information, please e-mail the Andrews McMeel Publishing Special Sales Department: specialsales@amuniversal.com.